Sight Words Secret Codes & Puzzles

Creative Activities That Teach the 50 Most Important Sight Words

by
Linda Standke

illustrated by
Julie Anderson

Key Education
An imprint of Carson-Dellosa Publishing, LLC
Greensboro, North Carolina

carsondellosa.com

Credits
Author: Linda Standke
Illustrator: Julie Anderson
Editors: Karen Seberg & Claude Chalk
Cover Photograph: © Digital Vision

Key Education
An imprint of Carson-Dellosa Publishing, LLC
PO Box 35665
Greensboro, NC 27425 USA
carsondellosa.com

ISBN 978-1-60268-060-9
04-179168091

Table of Contents

Sight Word Secret Codes & Puzzles

Student Sight Word Checklist

Student's Name:			Date 1:	Date 2:	Date 3:

☐☐☐ I	☐☐☐ here	☐☐☐ me
☐☐☐ a	☐☐☐ have	☐☐☐ find
☐☐☐ see	☐☐☐ my	☐☐☐ red
☐☐☐ like	☐☐☐ on	☐☐☐ blue
☐☐☐ the	☐☐☐ they	☐☐☐ yellow
☐☐☐ at	☐☐☐ are	☐☐☐ good
☐☐☐ look	☐☐☐ to	☐☐☐ funny
☐☐☐ you	☐☐☐ for	☐☐☐ make
☐☐☐ can	☐☐☐ said	☐☐☐ big
☐☐☐ and	☐☐☐ up	☐☐☐ little
☐☐☐ play	☐☐☐ down	☐☐☐ get
☐☐☐ is	☐☐☐ not	☐☐☐ did
☐☐☐ it	☐☐☐ this	☐☐☐ with
☐☐☐ in	☐☐☐ we	☐☐☐ ride
☐☐☐ go	☐☐☐ come	☐☐☐ jump
☐☐☐ he	☐☐☐ want	☐☐☐ help
☐☐☐ she	☐☐☐ run	

"I" Is a Letter and a Word

Trace the word "I."

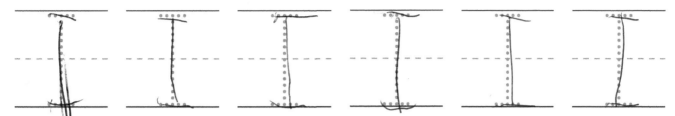

Print "I" on each line.

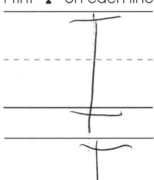

like you.

can see.

play.

like it.

Cut and paste the matching pictures.

"Aa" Is a Letter and a Word

Color the sections with "**A**" **red**.   Color the sections with "**a**" **green**.
Color the sections with "**▼**" **blue**.   What do you see?

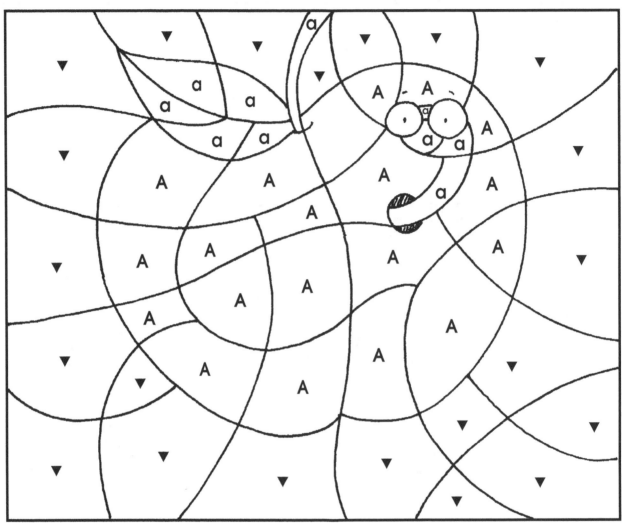

Trace "**A**" and "**a**."

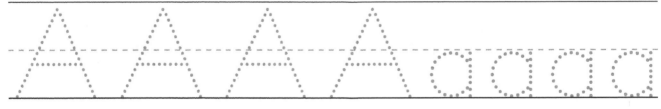

Print "**A**" and "**a**."

"See" the Sunglasses

Color the glasses that have two words that spell " see "

see   see

saw   see

see   see

see   see

see   see

set

see   eel

sun   see

see   see

see   see

Print the word "**see**."

7

I "Like" Ice Cream

Color the ice cream cones that have the word " like "

Print the word "**like**."

_____

_____

Look at "the" Train!

Color the train cars with the word "**the**."

toy   the   then   the

Trace the word "**the**."

Print the word "**the**."

Read and trace.

I see a

I like the

Help the frog hop across the pond.

"At" the Pond!

Draw a line to connect the lily pads that have the word "**at**." Color the frogs.

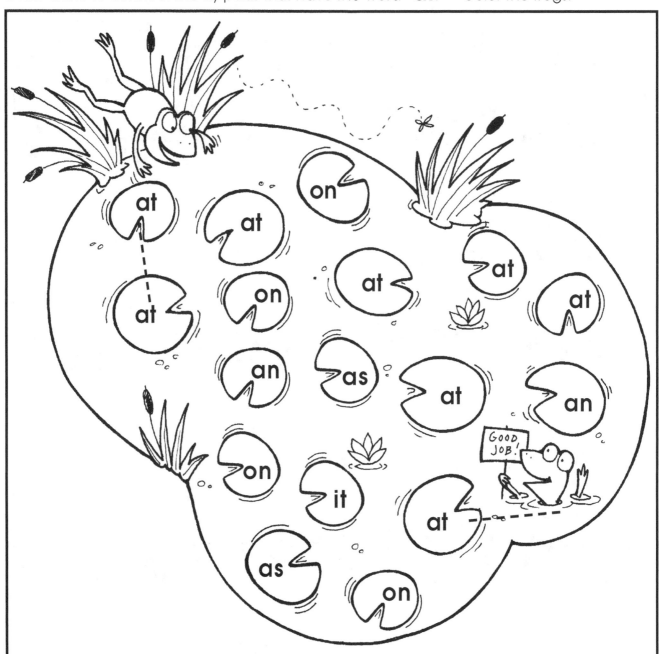

Print the word "**at**" on each lily pad.

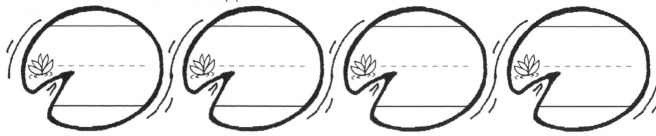

"Look" and Color!

Color the sections with a "●" **black**.

Color the sections with a "▲" **red**.

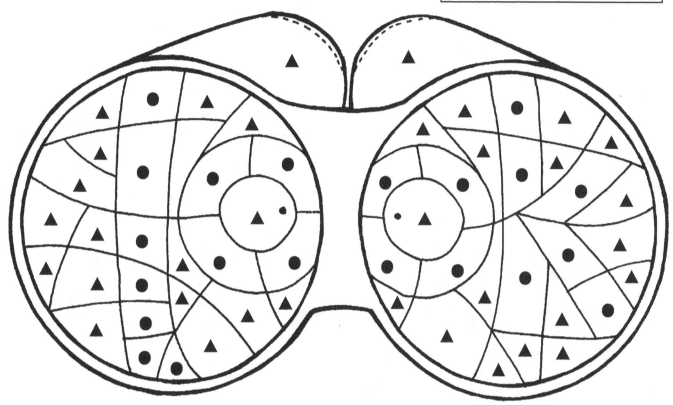

Trace the letters that spell "**look**."   Color the animals.

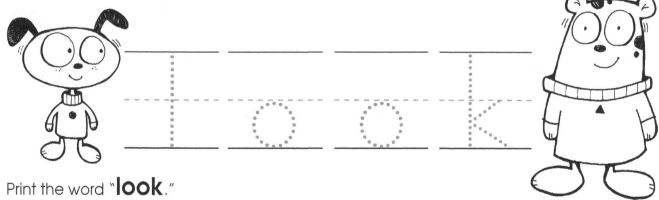

Print the word "**look**."

I Will Play with "You"

Help the children play catch with the balls.   Connect the balls that have the word "**you**."
Color the children.

Print the word "**you**."

you _____ _____ _____

"Can" You?

Print the missing letters to spell the word "**can**."

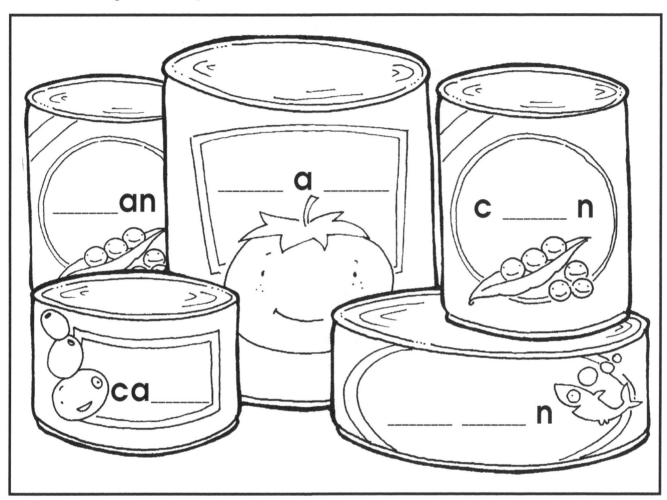

Trace the word "**can**."

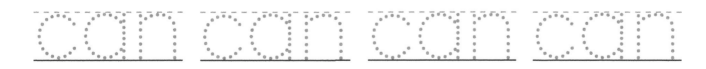

Print the word "**can**."

A Swinging Review!

Trace and print each word.   Color the picture.

the   look

can   you

O the words that are spelled correctly.   X the words that are spelled wrong.

Ipay (can) hte ouu aan you play the

the you yapl eht can yot play cae

Print "and" Cut "and" Paste

Print the word "**and**." Cut out each picture below.
Glue them next to their "go-together" pictures. Color the pictures.

	and	
	and	
	and	
	and	
	and	

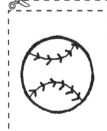

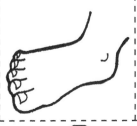

"Play" with Blocks

Cut out the letters below.   Glue them on the line of blocks that spell "**play**."

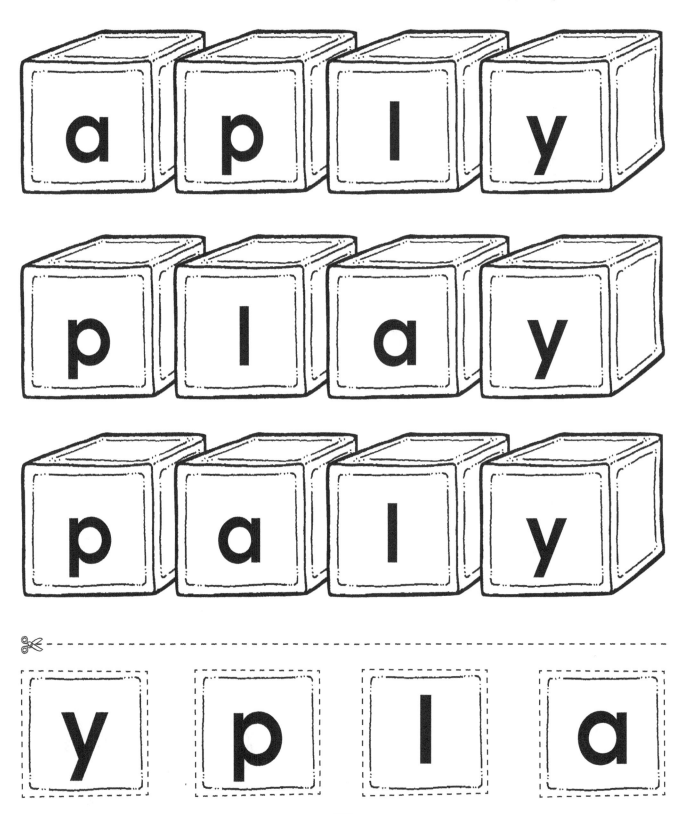

Three Little Words

Color the ✏️ with "**is**" red. Color the ✏️ with "**it**" blue. Color the ✏️ with "**in**" yellow.

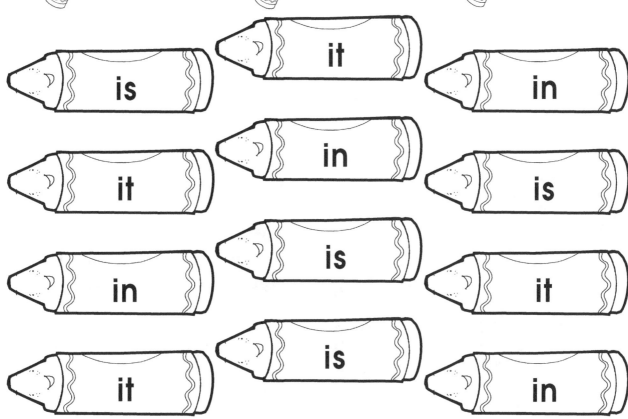

Trace the word "**is**."	Trace the word "**it**."	Trace the word "**in**."
is is is	it it it	in in in
Print the word "**is**."	Print the word "**it**."	Print the word "**in**."

"Go" "Go" "Go"!

Trace the word "**go**."

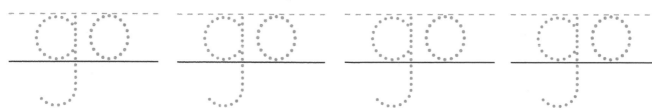

Print the missing letters to spell the word "**go**."

Print the word "**go**."

Word Search Review

Look at the word bank.
Find and circle the words in the puzzle.

i	s	i	n	c	a	n
p	l	a	y	u	f	q
x	i	t	o	x	g	o
x	k	x	u	x	i	t
s	e	e	u	a	n	d
k	c	a	t	f	h	I
l	o	o	k	t	h	e

Word Bank

play   you   like   look   go   I   and   at   see   it   can   is   in   the

Circle the word that is spelled correctly in each column.

like	pyal	olok	nda	nac
kile	play	loko	and	anc
elik	ylap	look	dna	can

Look At All the Boys!

he

Trace the word "**he**."

Print the word "**he**."

_____   _____   _____

_ _ _ _ _ _ _ _   _ _ _ _ _ _ _ _   _ _ _ _ _ _ _ _

_____   _____   _____

Name _____

Date _____

Lots of Girls!

Trace each girl's path.   Then, trace the word "**she**."   Color the girls.

Print the word "**she**."

KE-804074 © Carson-Dellosa

21

Sight Word Secret Codes & Puzzles

Look "Here"

Find and circle the word "**here**" five times.   Color the teacher.

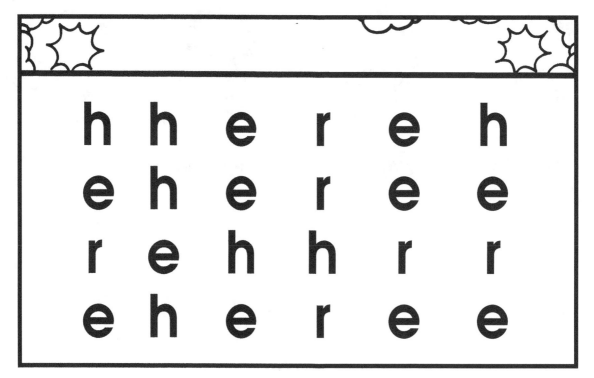

h	h	e	r	e	h
e	h	e	r	e	e
r	e	h	h	r	r
e	h	e	r	e	e

Trace the word "**here**."   Print the word "**here**."

here

here

here

I "Have" a Castle

Print the missing letters to spell the word "**have**."   Color the picture.

have

ha____e

h____ve

hav____

____ave

Print the word "**have**."

23

Where Is "My" Drink?

Color the drinks that have the word "**my**."

Trace the word "**my**."

my my

Print the word "**my**."

Ants "on" a Hill!

Color all the ants that have the word "**on**."

Trace the word "**on**." | Print the word "**on**."

Color Code

Color the sections with a "♥"red.   Color the sections with a "♦" blue.

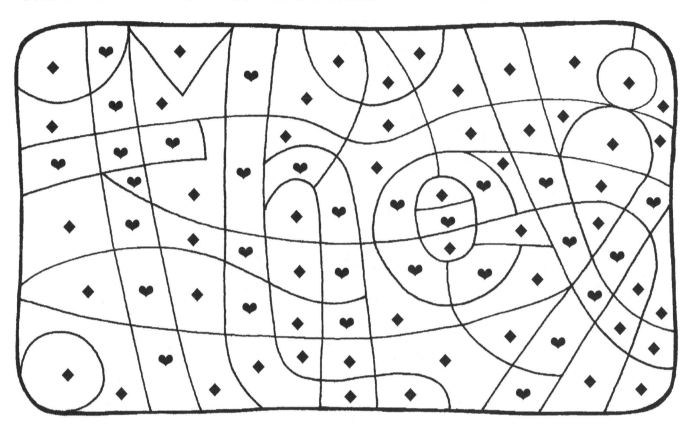

Trace the word "**they**."

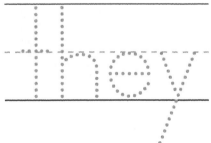 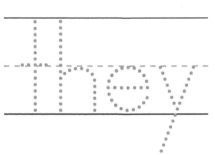

Print the word "**they**."

Name _____   Date _____

Word Search Review

Look at the word bank.   Find and circle the words in the puzzle.   Color the kids.

t	h	e	y	l	i	k	e
i	s	i	l	o	o	k	u
a	n	d	n	h	e	r	e
h	a	v	e	c	a	n	c
w	x	q	x	c	s	h	e
p	l	a	y	f	y	o	u
b	l	p	h	e	u	n	x
p	i	n	k	m	s	e	e

Word Bank

Print all the words that have an "a."

_____

_____

_____

_____

"Are" They Fishing?

Color the fish with the word "**are**" orange.   Color all the other fish **yellow**.   Color the boys.

are

Print the word "**are**."

_____

are _____

Trace the word "**to**."

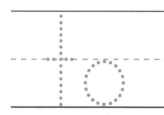

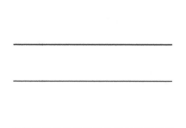

Print the word "**to**."

Time "to" Stop!

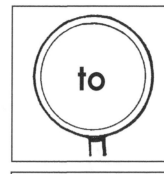

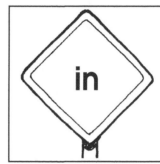

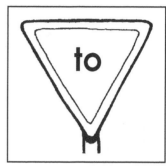

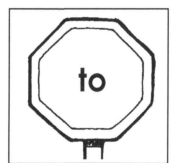

Directions:

Color and cut out the signs with the word "**to**."

Glue them to the matching signs above.

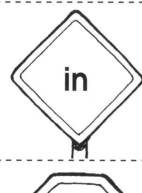

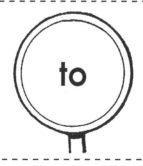

Name _____   Date _____

Ladybug, Ladybug!

Follow the ladybug along the path.   Circle all the words "**for**."   Color the picture.

Trace the word "**for**."   Print the word "**for**."

for   _____   _____

Buried Treasure Code

Use the code to print the word "**said**."   Color the jewels and treasure chest.

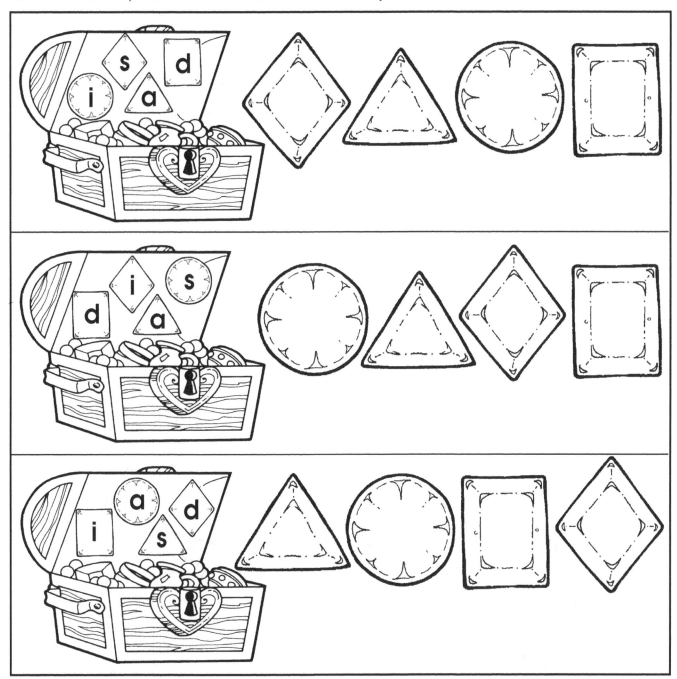

Trace the word "**said**."   Print the word "**said**."

said _____   _____

Name ______________________ Date ______________

Outer Space Code Review

Use the code below to fill in the missing letters. Print the words. Color the aliens.

___ ___   ___ ___   ___ ___
3 1   3 4   3 7

___ ___ ___ ___   ___ ___ ___ ___
11 0 9 8   4 5 2 8

___ ___ ___ ___   ___ ___ ___ ___
5 9 10 2   0 3 12 2

___ ___ ___   ___ ___ ___
9 7 6   1 2 2

___ ___ ___ ___
1 9 3 6

l	s	e	i	t	h	d		y	a	v		k
0	1	2	3	4	5	6	7	8	9	10	11	12

"Up" "Up" and Away!

On each balloon trace the word "**up**."   On each basket print the word "**up**."
Color the animals.

I am _____ in a balloon.

33

Name _____   Date _____

"Down" We Go!

On each slide, circle the letters that spell "**down**."

Color the children.

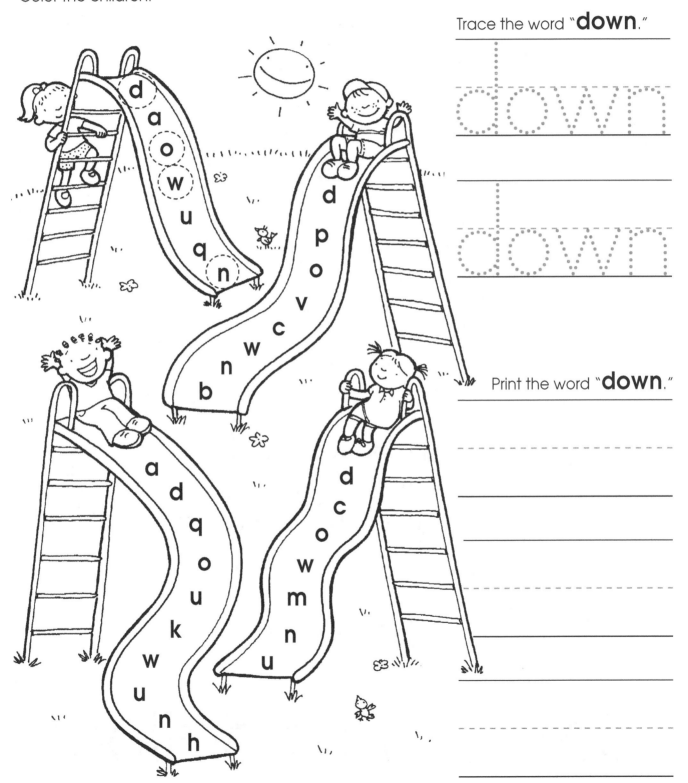

Trace the word "**down**."

Print the word "**down**."

"NOT"

Trace the word "**not**."

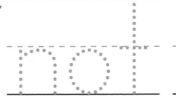

Print the word "**not**."

Directions:
1. Find and circle the letters that spell "**not**."

2. Draw a line through each tic-tac-toe!

out	owl	now
not	not	not
hot	net	got

out	no	not
now	owl	not
nut	out	not

"This" Way!

Follow the road and trace the letters that spell the word "**this**."

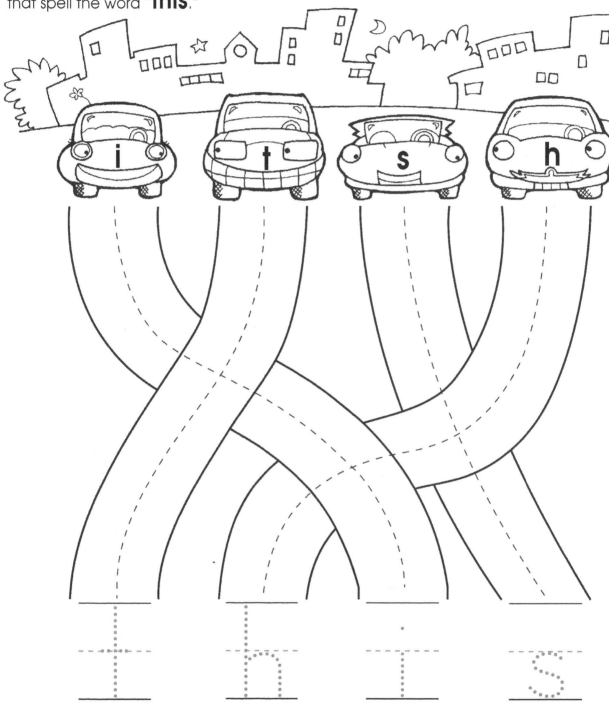

Print the word "**this**."

_____   _____   _____

- -

_____   _____   _____

Eight Crossword Review

Fill in the crossword puzzle using the words in the word bank.   Color the octopus.

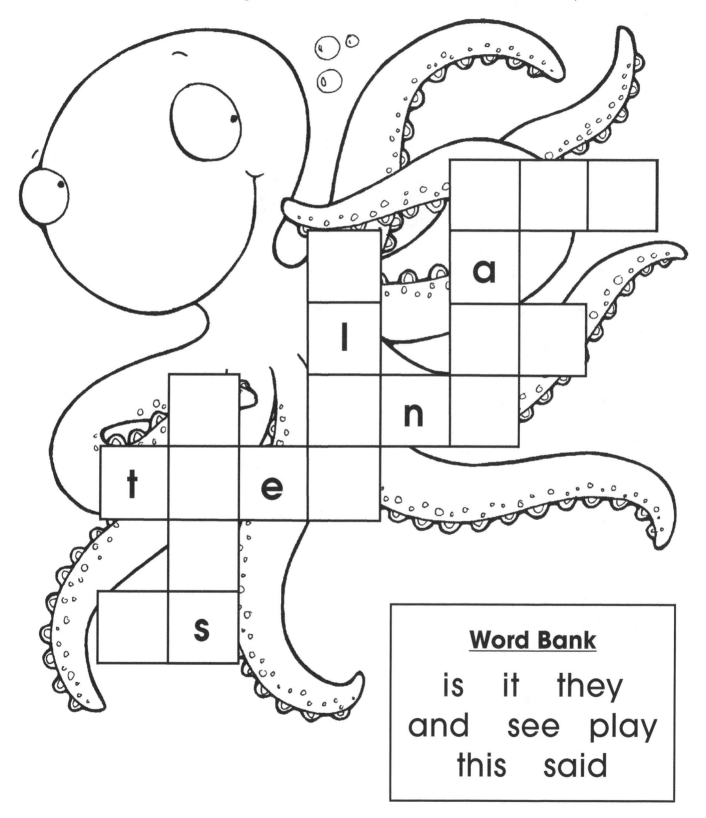

Word Bank

is   it   they

and   see   play

this   said

KE-804074 © Carson-Dellosa

Sight Word Secret Codes & Puzzles

"We" Are Friends!

Color the children who are holding the word "**we**."

Trace the word "**we**."

Print the word "**we**."

"Come" Crossword Puzzle

Trace the word "**come**."

Cut out the letters below.
Paste them in the boxes to
make the word "**come**."

come

come

		o		e

c		m	

| |
| e |

✂ -

c	o	o	o	m	m	e	e

I "Want" a Flower!

Finish the picture by connecting the letters that spell the word "**want**."

Trace the word
"**want**."

Print the word "**want**."

"Run" "Run" "Run"!

Trace the word "**run**."

r u n

r u n

r u n

run	run	run
row	rat	fun
ran	out	sun

Print the word "**run**."

ran	run	rut
row	run	fun
ran	run	rim

It's "Me"!

Color each child with the word "**me**."

Trace the word "**me**."

Print the word "**me**."

Review Very Little Words

Color the popcorn with words
from the word bank.

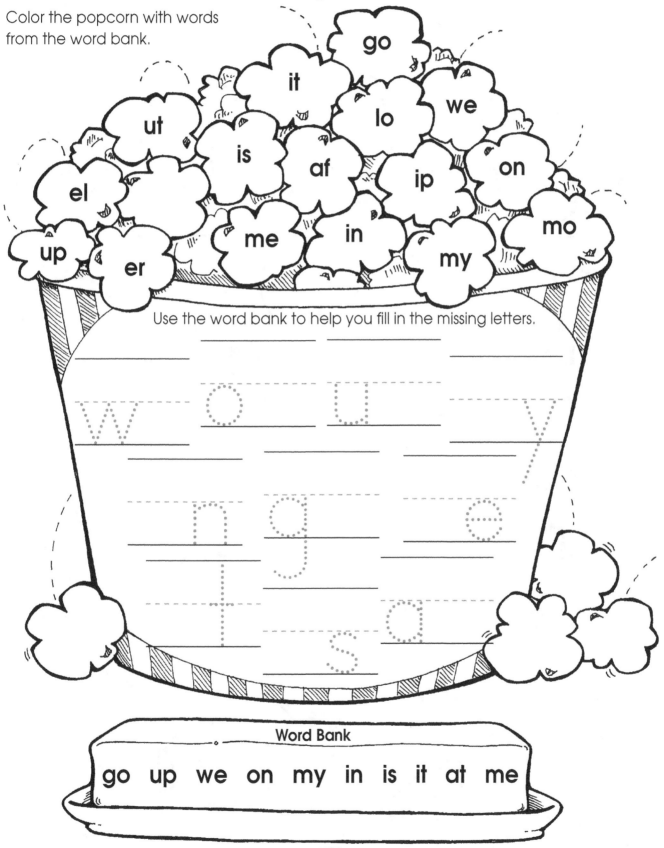

go

it

lo   we

ut

is   af   ip   on

el

me   in   mo

up   er   my

Use the word bank to help you fill in the missing letters.

_____   _____   _____

w   o   u   y

n   g   e

g

t   s   a

Word Bank

go   up   we   on   my   in   is   it   at   me

"Find" and Cut and Paste

Cut out the shapes at the bottom.   Glue them on the shapes that spell the word "**find**."

"Red" Balloons

Trace the letters that spell the word "**red**."

Then, trace the balloon strings to connect the letters.

Color the balloons with the word "**red**."

Trace the word "**red**."

Print the word "**red**."

"Blue" Birds

Print the word "**blue**" five times to finish the crossword puzzle.

Color the birds "**blue**."

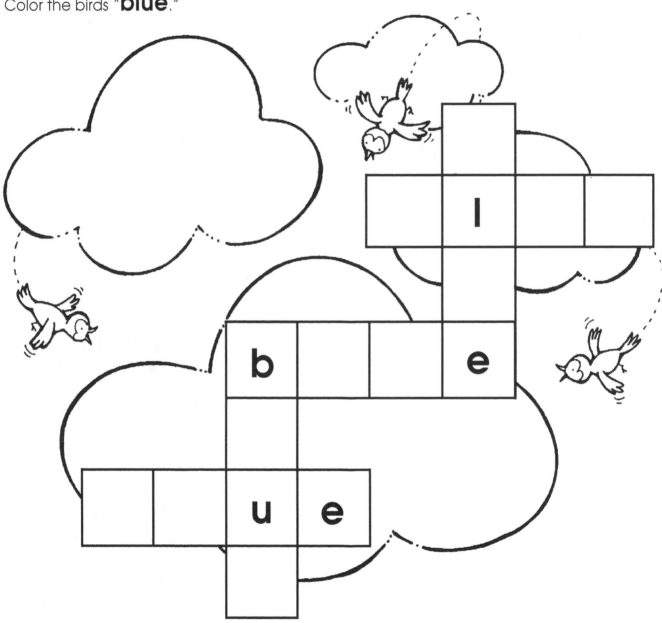

Trace the word "**blue**."

blue

blue

Find the Hidden Word

Color the sections with a "●" **yellow**.   Color the sections with a "■" **orange**.

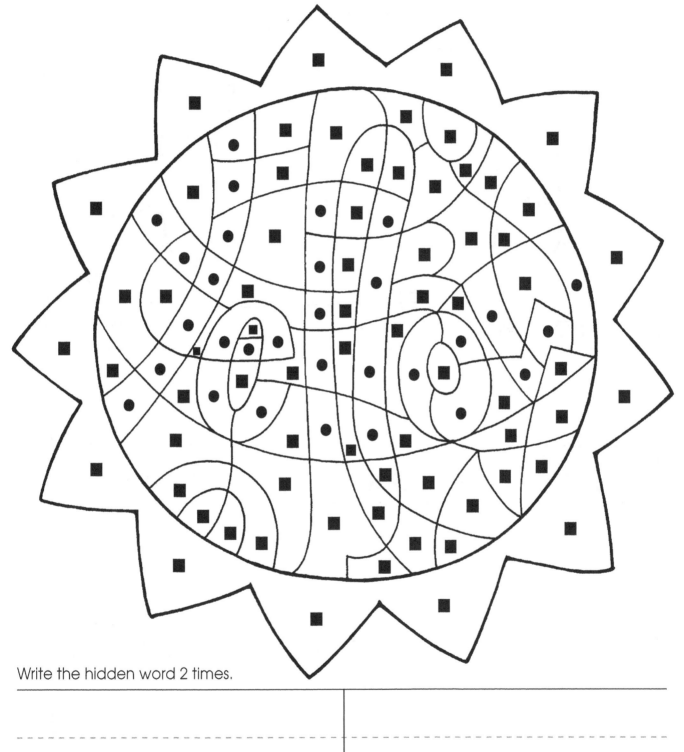

Write the hidden word 2 times.

_____ | _____

- - - - - - - - - - - - - - - | - - - - - - - - - - - - - - -

_____ | _____

Unlock the Words Review

Use the word bank to help you unscramble the words.

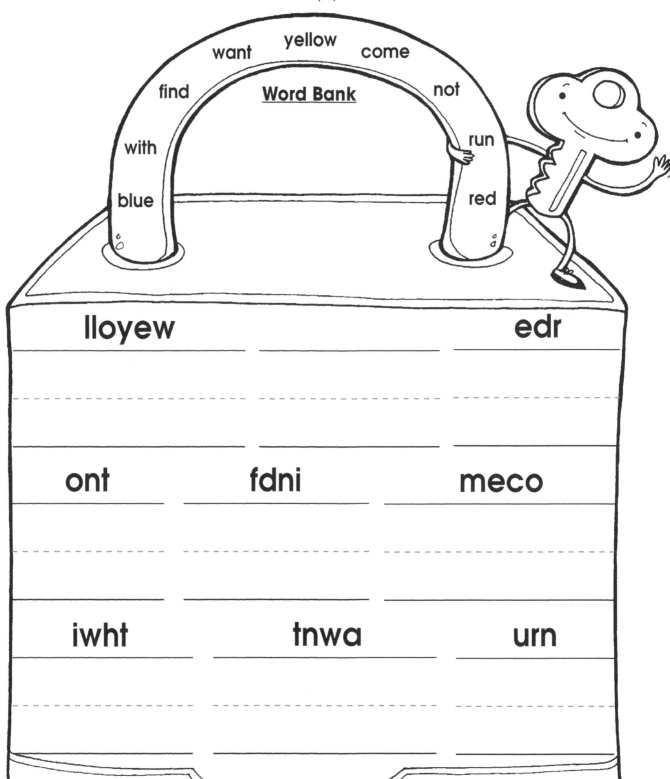

Word Bank

want yellow come find not with run blue red

lloyew _____   edr _____

ont _____   fdni _____   meco _____

iwht _____   tnwa _____   urn _____

Yummy "Good"!

Draw a line on each cookie to connect the letters that spell the word "**good**."
Color the cookies.

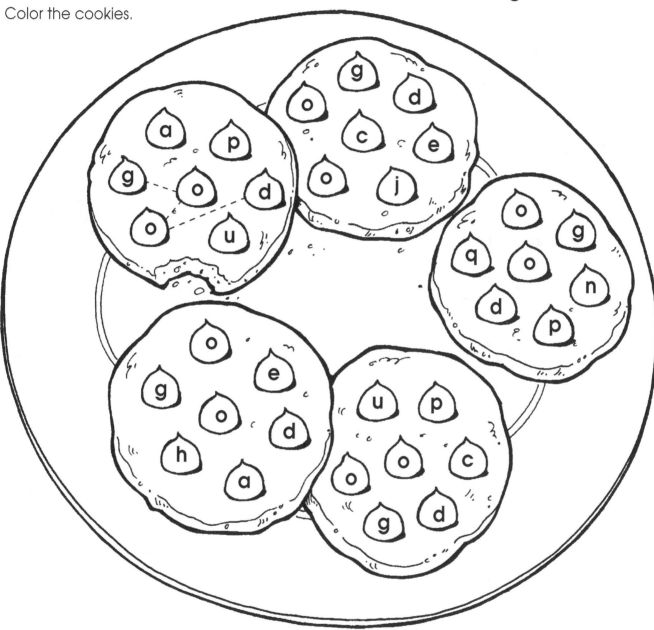

Trace the word "**good**."   Print the word "**good**."

good

Too "Funny"!

Draw a line to connect the faces that spell the word "**funny**."
Color the children.

Trace the word "**funny**."

Print the word "**funny**."

You Can "Make" a Goal!

Connect the soccer balls to spell the word "**make**." Color the children.

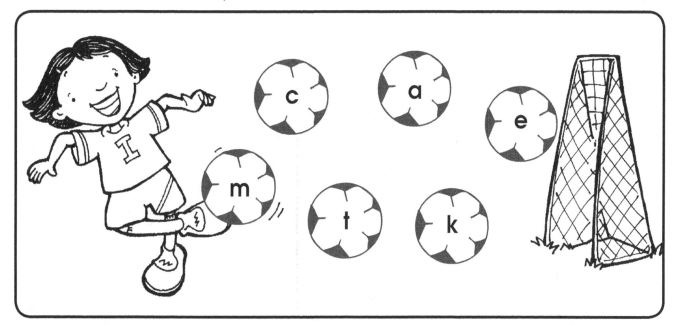

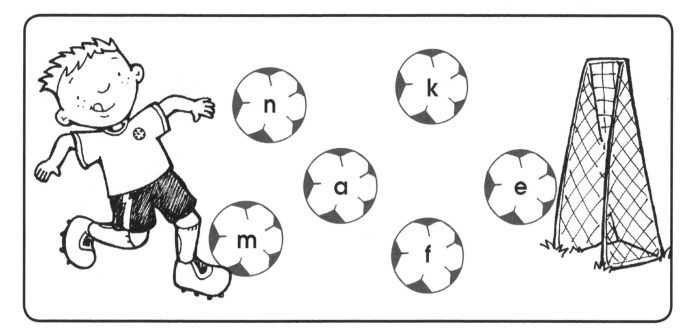

Trace the word "**make**." _____   Print the word "**make**." _____

make _____   _____

Get to the "Big" Robot

Follow the maze. Circle the words "**big**" to find your way to the "**big**" robot.

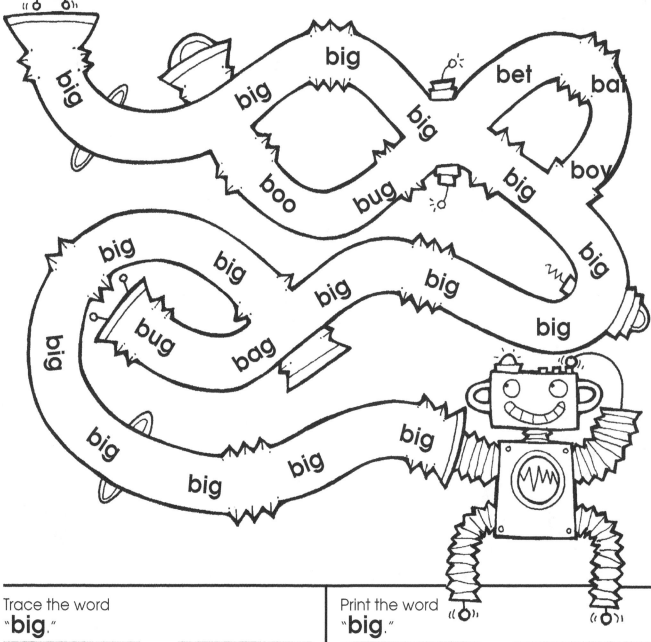

Trace the word "**big**."

big big

Print the word "**big**."

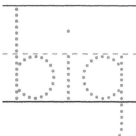

Duck, Duck, "Little" Duck!

Connect the ducks that spell the word "**little**."   Color all the ducks.

Trace the letters that spell the word "**little**."

_ _ _ _ _ _ _ _ _ _ _ _ _ _ _

Print the word "**little**."

Name _____ Date _____

"Get" the Little Worms!

Color the worms with the word "**get**." Color the big bird **blue**.
Color the little bird **yellow**.

Trace the word "**get**."

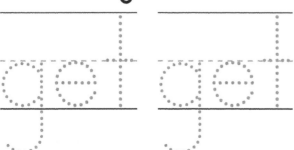

Print the word "**get**."

Name _____   Date _____

Building Blocks Review

Use the word bank below to unscramble the words.

 egt _____

 letlit _____

 ogdo _____

 akme _____

_____

 nnfuy _____

Draw a line to finish each word.
Use the word bank to help you.

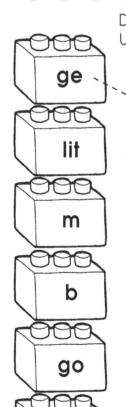
ge
lit
m
b
go
fun

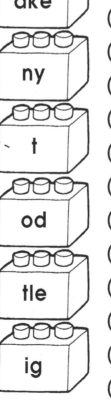
ake
ny
t
od
tle
ig

Word Bank
get
make
little
big
funny

Name _____ Date _____

How Many "Did" You Find?

The word "**did**" is hidden in the sidewalks.   Circle the letters that spell the word "**did**."

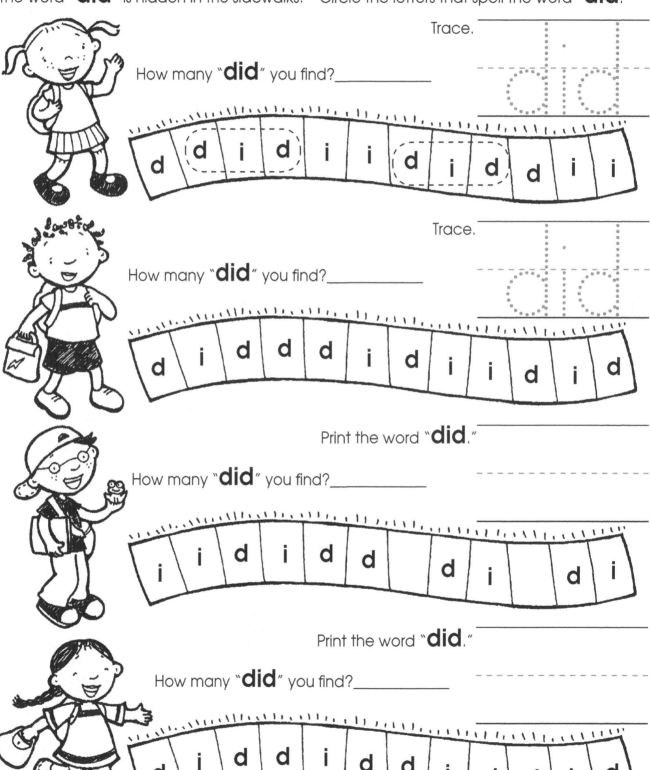

Trace.

How many "**did**" you find? _____

d d i d i i d i d d i i

Trace.

How many "**did**" you find? _____

d i d d d i d i i d i d

Print the word "**did**."

How many "**did**" you find? _____

i i d i d d d i d i

Print the word "**did**."

How many "**did**" you find? _____

d i d d d i d d i d i d

Break the Shape Code

Trace the word "**with**." Use the code in each box. Then, write the word.

Print the word "**with**."

Name _____   Date _____

"Ride" That Pony!

Finish the picture.   Connect the letters to spell the word "**ride**."   Color the picture.

Trace the word "**ride**."

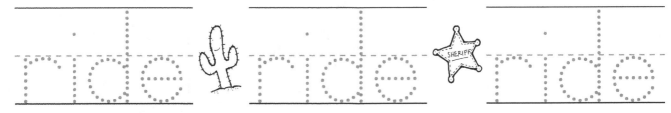

Print the word "**ride**."

_____   _____

_____   _____   _____

Name _____   Date _____

"Jump" for Joy!

Circle the words "**jump**."   Color the children.

jet

jump   jump   jump

jump

pump   jack

jump   just

jump   jump

jump   jump

Trace the word "**jump**."   Print the word "**jump**."

"Help" Rake the Yard!

Circle the hidden letters that spell the word "**help**."   Color the picture.

Trace the word "**help**."

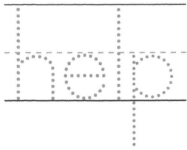   help   help

Print the word "**help**."

_____   _____   _____

- - - - - - - - - - -   - - - - - - - - - - -   - - - - - - - - - - -

_____   _____   _____

Secret Code Review

Use the code below. Print the words.

a	d		h	i	j	l	m	n	o	p	r	t	u	w
➼	✧		▲	○	✖	✳	✿	●	☆	▢	◆	★	✈	♥	■

Answer Key

Pages 5–18
Check children's work.

Top of page 19

Bottom of page 19

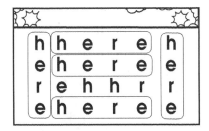

like	pyal	olok	nda	nac
kile	play	loko	and	anc
elik	ylap	look	dna	can

Pages 20–21
Check children's work.

Page 22

h	h	e	r	e	h
e	e	h	e	r	e
r	e	h	h	r	r
e	e	h	e	r	e

Pages 23–26
Check children's work.

Top of page 27

t	h	e	y	l	i	k	e
i	s	i	l	o	o	k	u
a	n	d	n	h	e	r	e
h	a	v	e	c	a	n	e
w	g	q	x	c	s	h	e
p	l	a	y	f	y	o	u
b	l	p	h	e	u	n	x
p	i	n	k	m	s	e	e

Bottom of page 27

they play can
have and

Pages 28–31
Check children's work.

Page 32

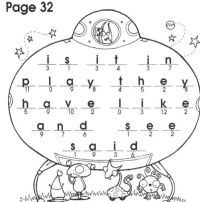

i s i t i n
3 1 3 4 1 7

p l a y t h e y
11 7 9 8 7 5 2 8

h a v e l i k e
5 9 10 2 3 1 8 2

a n d s e e
9 7 6 1 2 2

s a i d
1 9 3 6

Pages 33–34
Check children's work.

Page 35

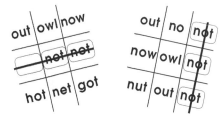

out owl now
not not
hot net got

out no not
now owl not
nut out not

Page 36
Check children's work.

Page 37

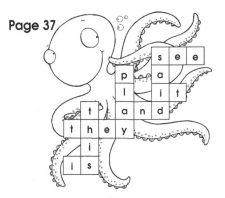

Page 38
Check children's work.

Page 39

Page 40
Check children's work.

Page 41

run	run	run
row	rat	fun
ran	out	sun

ran	run	rut
row	run	fun
ran	run	rim

Pages 42
Check children's work.

Pages 43

we on up my
in go me
it is at

Pages 44–45
Check children's work.

Answer Key

Page 46

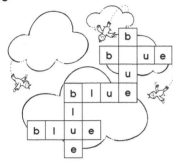

Page 47
Check children's work.

Page 48

Pages 49–51
Check children's work.

Page 52

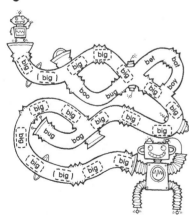

Pages 53–54
Check children's work.

Top of page 55

get   little
good   make
big   funny

Bottom of page 55

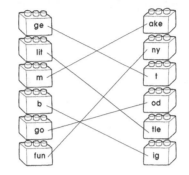

ge   ake
lit   ny
m   t
b   od
go   tle
fun   ig

Pages 56

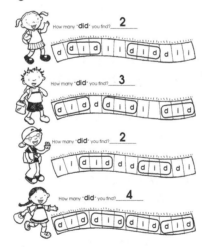

How many "did" you find? __2__

How many "did" you find? __3__

How many "did" you find? __2__

How many "did" you find? __4__

Pages 57–59
Check children's work.

Page 60

Page 61

help   to
want   up
jump
ride   we

Correlations to NCTE/IRA Standards and NAEYC/IRA Position Statement

Sight Word Secret Codes & Puzzles supports the NCTE/IRA *Standards for the English Language Arts* and the recommended teaching practices outlined in the NAEYC/IRA position statement *Learning to Read and Write: Developmentally Appropriate Practices for Young Children.*

NCTE/IRA *Standards for the English Language Arts*

Each activity in this book supports one or more of the following standards:

1. **Students read many different types of print and nonprint texts for a variety of purposes.** Students read a variety of sight words while ding the activities in this book.

2. **Students use a variety of strategies to build meaning while reading.** The activities in this book promote sight word recognition, an essential skill in learning to read.

3. **Students communicate in spoken, written, and visual form, for a variety of purposes and a variety of audiences.** In *Sight Word Secret Codes & Puzzles*, students write sight words and communicate visually through coloring and cut-and-paste activities to support their learning of sight words and to show what they have learned.

NAEYC/IRA Position Statement *Learning to Read and Write: Developmentally Appropriate Practices for Young Children*

This book and the activities in it support the following recommended teaching practices for kindergarten and primary-grade students:

1. **Teachers read to children daily and provide opportunities for students to read independently both fiction and nonfiction texts.** In *Sight Word Secret Codes & Puzzles*, students read letters and words in order to learn sight words.

2. **Teachers provide opportunities for students to write many different kinds of texts for different purposes.** Students learn to write a variety of sight words through the activities in this book.

3. **Teachers provide challenging instruction that expands children's knowledge of their world and expands their vocabularies.** *Sight Word Secret Codes & Puzzles* helps expand children's vocabularies by introducing 50 essential sight words.